No greater love, unquestioning, undemanding;
no greater trust and loyalty to the end will be shown to man
than by his greatest friend – his dog.

But within man lies a cruel streak
and not always is the friendship returned.....

It is left up to a true animal lover to provide that second chance.

REX : *A Happy Breed Rescue Dog*

ANOTHER CHANCE

Claire McClennan

With Drawings by
Linda Thurlow

HOLROCKS BOOKS

First published in 1997 by HolRocks Books
PO Box 107
Paignton
Devon
TQ4 7YR

ANOTHER CHANCE

A CIP catalogue record for this book
is available from the British Library

ISBN 0 -9526944 -1 -7

Typeset, Printed and Bound in Great Britain
by The Lazarus Press
6 Grenville Street
Bideford
Devon EX39 2EA

'If a very small rescue can make a tiny ripple
in the large pond of unwanted animals,
by finding a secure and loving home for just one,
then we feel it's a worthwhile cause.'

Maria Goodman
Sylphlyke Animal Sanctuary

CONTENTS

CONTENTS

MR. HOPEFUL

The Unknown Mongrel

§

A black, moist nose pushes through the bars,
Behind sad eyes lies the truth, the scars.
At ten years old, age is not on his side,
Long gone his sparkle and sense of pride.
He droops his tail, hangs his head in shame,
No-one bothers to stop to ask his name.
A typical cross-breed, he'll be passed by
A pedigree pup will catch your eye.
He's lived at the rescue three years or more,
If only you'd notice, he'd offer a paw.
All he needs is that chance, a chance to re-live,
To be your best friend, his love to give.
Please stop! Turn around, take a second glance
Give that unknown mongrel *Another Chance.*

C.M.

QUINCY

A Golden Retriever, scalded and turned out into the streets.
Classed as 'cosmetically unacceptable'
– nobody wanted to know.
He became SSPCA Chief Inspector Iain Keir's
'special rescue'.

Late one August night in 1983 Golden Retriever Quincy, approximately three years old, sat terrified in the Stolen Goods Compound of the local Police Station in Hamilton. A call was made by the Police through to Chief Inspector Keir at the Scottish SPCA – an injured dog needed help.

The night was warm and hanging in a dark sky there was a full moon which lit up the wire enclosed compound at the rear of the Station's office. Inside stood the large Golden Retriever, watching warily as Chief Inspector Keir approached talking quietly and reassuringly. The only movement from the dog was a gentle wagging of the tip of his tail and slowly he allowed himself to be led from the compound into a lighted office. Only then did the full state of his injuries become truly apparent. Even to an SSPCA Inspector who often witnessed much tragedy, the injuries on this dog were 'horrific'.

His head, muzzle and parts of his back were red raw – inflamed and weeping – fringed with matted hair and dead skin. Someone had thrown scalding water on top of the Retriever's head for whatever reason and scarred him for life. (Despite a full investigation by Police and SSPCA officials, the perpetrator was never found, nor did an owner ever come forward.) Only by sheer good fortune were his eyes not affected. He had then been turned out onto the streets and left to roam in agony.

For three long hours Chief Inspector Keir, helped by a local vet, worked on the dog's head, sterilising and cleaning the wounds, cutting away matted hair and dead skin. The most

3

awkward part was removing the small grass seeds that had become embedded in the dog's skin as he had rubbed his injured head in the grass to try to relieve the pain and in his helpless effort to clean himself. The Chief Inspector estimated that his accident must have taken place the previous weekend which meant the dog had been hiding from human contact for at least six days – doing what injured animals do – lying up, trusting that God and nature would repair the damage.

Throughout the cleaning of his face, the dog never once growled or threatened. He suffered his pain in silence. Occasionally, he would expel his breath in an exasperated way. 'Well, three hours sitting still is a very long time!' explains Inspector Keir. 'Occasionally he would turn to nudge away with his nose a hand that was inadvertently causing discomfort.'

After antibiotic injections and liberal applications of soothing cream, Iain took him home and bedded him down in his kitchen.

The following day Iain took the dog to the SSPCA's Animal Welfare Centre where, for the next five weeks, the Retriever received daily veterinary attention, many liberal coatings of ointment to his sore parts and lots of tender, loving care. But he was not alone. He had found one true friend in the form of hard working Chief Inspector Keir. Each day he visited him at the Centre, assisting with his treatment but also walking him around the large tree lined paddock which is where true bonding and rapport developed. Iain says, 'The wonderment of it all was that he seemed to hold no grudge against humans. He just loved all people!'

Within a few weeks the dog was on the road to recovery, given the 'all clear' by the vet and available for a new home. He had proved himself to be a gentle, friendly Retriever, lovable and affectionate, with the best of natures towards humans and other animals.

But after three weeks of trying, there were simply no takers. He had been left with physical scars. With a bald, scarred fore-

'I'll be your friend, Quincy.' Chief Inspector Keir saw beyond Quincy's facial injuries and became his best friend.

head he found himself classed as 'cosmetically unacceptable'.

There were many visitors to the Centre looking for an animal to take home as a pet. Usually there would be no problem re-homing an affectionate Golden Retriever. But not one single person picked this one. Quite simply, no-one could see beneath his scars. He was not wanted. He was doomed to be humanely destroyed.

Chief Inspector Keir had vowed he would not have another dog after he had lost his much loved Collie. But he knew if he did not adopt this one.....

The two were already 'best of friends' and he decided, along with his wife, that this dog was 'extra special'. They chose to make him one of their family, much to the delight of their son and daughter.

The family named him 'Quincy' after the television character. 'He was not very handsome but loveable, intelligent and a trier!' Their two rescued cats, Fudge and Muffin, after walking on the higher furniture for about three weeks, gradually accepted him, came back down to earth and were good pals thereafter. Fred, the family Macaw, occasionally had a go at nibbling Quincy's tail, much to the dog's amusement and friendly Quincy soon got to know the local children when he accompanied his new master to the primary schools for talks. Says Iain, 'It was nice to be known as "The Man with the Baldy Dog!".'

In 1987, due to an injury, Quincy had to have his tail docked. His lovely feathers were gone but he was still his old lovable self. Any birds and small animals which his master brought home were sniffed, licked and generally watched over by Quincy who could be relied upon to show Iain the way when one chose to hide out in the garden shrubbery.

Over the years Quincy's greatest love was to accompany his master in the van on night emergency calls. When the telephone rang, he would look around and by the time Iain had his tunic on, Quincy was standing by the door ready to go to work! No-one was allowed to join him in the vehicle except 'his dad'!

The two were BEST FRIENDS for almost nine wonderful years.

When Quincy's health deteriorated rapidly, making him a shadow of his former old self, he was gently put to sleep and buried in one of his favourite corners at the Animal Centre.

Quincy could have ended up a stray, scarred for life, a dog destroyed because nobody wanted to know, despite his good nature shining through his scars.

But in the words of his true friend Chief Inspector Iain Keir, 'Quincy was a special rescue, a saved soul. Thank you Quincy for being part of our family and giving us nine years of happiness. You didn't know that you weren't pretty – and we didn't care.'

ZUZU

Destined to die at the hands of pet flesh dealers
in mainland China.
An IFAW Co-Ordinator faced court prosecution
but successfully saved this little Terrier.

The International Fund for Animal Welfare South East Asia Co-ordinator David Dawson, his wife and a colleague were documenting animal abuse in Quinpong Market in Southern China. Reports had come to them, from IFAW supporters of terrible cruelty in butchering animals for human consumption.

The market had been described as a mixture of zoo slaughterhouse and torture chamber. A large variety of animals could be found there – dead owls and snakes, otters and deers, cats and dogs, pelts of animals such as leopards – a species threatened with extinction.

Animals were being slaughtered on the spot in an horrific manner and having just seen a live cat being dumped into boiling water, David came face to face with a terrified little bundle of a dog – waiting to die. Her pleading expression said all that needed to be said.

The little dog, about eighteen months old, a larger than average Tibetan Terrier, was the next in the queue to be killed. She reminded David so much of his own pet who had so recently died. The market dealer explained, in his simple language, the dog's fate and pulled his finger across his throat to emphasise the point.

David knew that saving one dog, amongst so many, would make little difference in the long run. He later said, 'It was illogical to rescue individual animals on emotional grounds. It doesn't help the campaign to save all animals in the future. It simply widens the market and creates space for another dog.'

But this was an occasion when quite simply he could not

walk past on the other side. 'This one dog symbolised what we were trying to do,' he said. 'If we couldn't save her, we couldn't save any.' David's wife Alex needed no time for consideration. Her mind was made up – she would save that little Terrier no matter what it took!

Much debate and argument later, the dealer was finally persuaded to part with the quivering, shaking dog, probably the only dog to come out of that market alive. He was paid £45 – equal to two weeks' takings for a market trader.

David and Alex immediately gave the terrified little creature a name – Zuzu. It was the first name that came into their heads as they took her away and also since she looked the image of their previous Beardie cross Ziggy. David obtained an official export license and a delighted David and Alex flew with their new little friend and the IFAW team on to Hong Kong.

But once in Hong Kong, Customs Officers claimed the correct procedures for importing an animal had not been followed. It was suggested that Zuzu might have to be destroyed and David was warned he faced prosecution.

In no time at all, David found himself in Court on charges of attempting to smuggle a dog into Hong Kong. To this he pleaded 'Guilty'. At the end of the case the Judge stated: 'Now I have heard the full facts, I would like to give you an absolute discharge but the law has been changed and no longer allows me to do this. I am therefore forced to impose a fine.... £1.41!'

The whole episode was a traumatic experience for the IFAW team but they had no regrets. Zuzu had been saved from a terrible fate. She flew to England and came out of quarantine with her little head held up high to become David and Alex's much loved family pet.

The Chinese Authorities duly received the IFAW reports on the horrific market activities and officials in Guangzhou are clamping down on the trading of protected animals and skins and the appalling treatment of cats and dogs destroyed for dinner tables. Dog is still a regular part of the diet in Southern

China and many are bred for the markets there. The 'eating' dogs are normally large Chows and are slaughtered away from the markets. Pet keeping is banned in the region but as Zuzu had arrived at the market alive, David reckons she was probably someone's pet, enforced by the fact she was wearing a collar and she had very soft pads on her paws.

The mission of IFAW is to promote and ensure 'the just and kind treatment of animals worldwide from bees to whales, pet puppies to dingoes, the beautiful and the ugly, the great and the small.'

Zuzu turned into a great family pet. A little dog with a great character, full of life and fun. She would run around continually nipping male ankles – 'A little revenge, I think, for what was done to her!' says David. She immediately became extremely affectionate to her new family. She adored David's other dog, a gentle giant of a Hong Kong stray called Joss; a wolf look-alike yet the gentlest of dogs, although fiercely defensive of everyone in her pack.

'Whenever Zuzu got into scrapes with other dogs – which happened frequently – Joss would be there to sort out the problem for her!' says David. 'One very lucky little Terrier!'

ZUZU : *Safely rescued from pet-flesh dealers by the Dawson family*

LESTER

A Greyhound, cast aside and dumped to become
a pitiful skeleton. Found love and affection at
THE PINE RIDGE DOG SANCTUARY.

In May 1992, a 'pitiful skeleton of a hunched up creature', picked up by a Berkshire Dog Warden, turned up on the doorstep of The Pine Ridge Dog Sanctuary. He was a young, red, brindle Greyhound, only five or six months old. As soon as the Sanctuary saw him, they knew he had little chance of being claimed, let alone of finding a new home.

Greyhounds are the sort of breed particularly difficult to re-home because, despite being very gentle pets, they are not the 'appealing dog' families are looking for. There is never any chance of tracking down the original heartless owner of a dog that has been dumped.

This particular Greyhound was quite simply starved and hairless, skin and bone. He had been dumped unloved in the Slough area where so often the local Dog Warden finds Greyhounds, unwanted because maybe they have suffered injuries or more often they are found to be just not fast enough on the track. If a dog is a winner, it becomes a hero. It becomes big business and the owner can make thousands of pounds. But a racing Greyhound's life is very short – four years if they are lucky but very often a racing career is cut short by injury. The sharp turns on the racetrack can so easily damage the animal's leg joints. Then, with a kind owner – there are too few of these – the dog will be kept on as a family pet or found another good home, but far more often of more importance, is the purchase of the next 'winner'. The unwanted Greyhound, still a young dog, is cast aside. Outside the bright lights and excitement of the circuit these dogs face a bleak future. They are left to wander the streets and roadside alone. Some do not even have security for

Mrs Connie Cuff of Pine Ridge (whose late husband Bernard Cuff received the ProDog National Charity Award for 'Outstanding Services to the World of Dogs') gave her time to Lester on his road to recovery

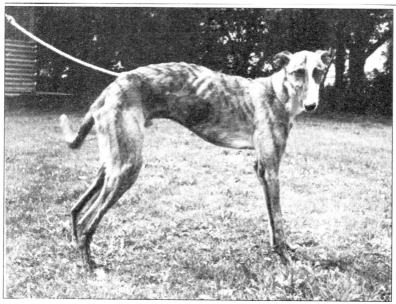

LESTER : *One of the luckier Greyhounds with a good future in front of him*

four years. If a dog does not measure up to expectation and show potential as a future winner in his initial trials, he could well be abandoned at the start.

Quiet and subdued, used to little food, this particular Greyhound, on this May day, simply put his life in the hands of Connie Cuff, Principal of Pine Ridge. She named him – Lester. He was wormed, given a gradual build up of a good diet and exercise and gradually the true hound began to emerge – a lively outgoing dog, sweet and gentle natured, who liked nothing better than to dribble his ball! Mixing playfully with all the other rescued dogs, his red, brindle coat picked up a wonderful shine and he was ready for a new home full of warmth and love – something he was obviously starved of in his early days.

It is the dogs at Pine Ridge who are there the longest, the noble ex-racing Greyhounds or the older dogs, that tend to capture the hearts of the Sanctuary workers. Seeing Greyhounds like Lester, day after day, just waiting behind the wire with pleading eyes for someone to pick them as the 'special one'.

Thousands of Greyhounds are bred in the United Kingdom each year, many more coming over from a large breeding centre in Ireland. Thousands of these retire when they are four-years-old. No wonder Greyhounds, through no fault of their own, jostle and juggle for places in animal rescue centres. Everything seems to point against the breed and many stay in the rescue centres for life. But when the right person does eventually come along, it makes it all the more rewarding for the hard working staff, as they know Greyhounds can be very suitable as family pets, ideal with children and very docile.

'That day did indeed come for Lester,' says Connie. 'We found him his own safe, loving home with three other dogs, four cats, three horses and several rabbits! With his horrendous puppy days well behind him, he makes the most of a wonderful life.'

Outside the bright lights of the race circuit,
Greyhounds face a very bleak future

KELLY

An Old English Sheepdog, 12 years of age.
Her coat matted to her body of skin and bone.
Had no such thing as exercise —
her owner 'didn't believe in leads'.
RSPCA Liverpool Branch came to her rescue.

As soon as any kind of animal atrocity is reported, the RSPCA are quick to step in. In May '91 their Liverpool branch received a call to visit the home of a Widnes labourer and his family.

RSPCA Inspector, Martin Marsh arrived at the home to find Kelly, an Old English Sheepdog, outside in the garden. She was in the most appalling condition. As he approached her, he noticed her eyes, full of abandonment. Her filthy, stringy coat clung to her body. It had been left to grow until it was matted, covered her eyes and clogged up her rear end. It was encrusted with flea dirt and her own excrement.

Beneath her coat she was clearly emaciated. Her body was so starved of food that her bones protruded through her shaggy coat. She was totally lifeless and sensitive to the touch. In Inspector Marsh's words: 'All the fire had gone out of her.'

'She is in a bit of a state' were the words used by the owner when he was confronted and he added that his family were going to contact the RSPCA because 'they thought the dog needed putting down'. He claimed Kelly, believed to be twelve-years-old, had been his dog for eight years. In all that time, she had never been to a vet and she was banished outside to the garden whatever the weather. He admitted he had not exercised his dog for 'a very long time'. He had never put her on a lead. 'I don't believe in them,' he said.

This owner claimed that on one occasion Kelly had gone for his wife and he feared she might bite someone else. His wife admitted she was very wary of going near the dog and as a

KELLY : *Standing lifeless, her bones protruding through her shaggy, overgrown coat*

result Kelly was rarely handled or given any kind of attention.

When the couple were asked if they were aware of how thin their dog had become, the owner's reply was : 'I've never really noticed.' He went on to say that they had considered handling Kelly into a Police Station and pretending she was a stray.

The couple were subsequently prosecuted for causing unnecessary suffering to their animal. They offered no defence to their actions and were fined £350 plus costs and banned for life from keeping any future dogs.

Despite the tremendous trauma for a twelve-year-old dog to go through, Old English Kelly amazingly survived her ordeal. She was immediately signed over into RSPCA care and was taken to a veterinary surgeon for immediate treatment. Once there, the full extent of her horrifying ordeal became apparent. She weighed just 14 Kg. Because of the state of her coat, she had to be completely stripped – it took two people all morning to strip the coat – and when the clogged matts of fur were removed, she was just skin and bone; her skin flakey, dry and sore. 'It was a miracle she could even stand,' said Inspector Marsh.

Throughout the clipping, Kelly showed not one ounce of aggression and could not have been more co-operative throughout the whole of her treatment. She must have known she was in hands that cared.

Off she then went to an RSPCA care home, was given a proper diet, gained a further 5 Kg. in the first month and with lots of love and affection became brighter and more alert.

It was here that Kelly found herself new, caring owners. A couple were visiting the Dogs Home with their other dog – also rescued from the RSPCA – and seeing Kelly in the corner of the kennel whimpering quietly, their heart's just went straight out to her.

It took a good few weeks, after such a lifetime experience, for Kelly to settle into her new home. She cowered whenever her new owners went into the garden, wondering whether she was going to be left outside as she had been for most of her life. But her new owners took her everywhere, calming her and flooding her with all the love and attention she had previously missed out on.

In time they were rewarded. Within a year, Kelly had fully recovered. Enjoying her retirement, she had become a changed animal, spoilt rotten and despite her old age, she showed loyalty and love in return to her devoted family.

KELLY : *On her way to a full recovery*

MAX

With a devoted owner, Max was the perfect puppy –
until he turned extremely aggressive. His owner
tried everything, but in vain. An Animal Behaviourist,
with dedication and understanding, shows how Max earned
himself another chance with his owner.

A growing number of people suffer behavioural problems with
their dogs. Many will cast aside these dogs, along with
the problems. They can not be bothered and they can not find
the time and effort it requires to find a solution. But many
quite simply are not aware they can do anything to improve the
situation.

When Erica Peachey, a member of the Association of Pet
Behaviour Counsellors, sees dog owners, she is very often the
last resort before the owners part with their dogs. With both
total dedication and full understanding of the dog, she can offer
that vital last chance.

Once such dog was Max, an eighteen-month-old German
Shepherd. His owner, Angela Hudson, contacted Erica in
desperation. Angela was an extremely caring owner, who had
done everything right with her dog but had still ended up with
problems she could not control.

She had bought Max as a puppy and had worked hard with
him, attending a dog club religiously since he was fourteen-
weeks-old. He was given two good walks a day and had the
companionship of an older dog who shared their home.

Angela was devoted to Max and he seemed like the perfect
dog. Which he was – until he saw another dog. Then Max
turned. His character changed and aggression raged. If he was
on the lead, he would bark and scream. If he was off the lead,
he would race in and bite.

A desperate Angela tried EVERYTHING! She repeated

ERICA PEACHEY :
Amongst her friends

MAX : *With much hard work from an Animal Behaviourist
Max earned himself his chance.*

everything she was told to do by trainers and the whole host of well-meaning people who appear with advice when a problem arises. Everything from castration to shouting at Max, to feeding him titbits. But Max's behaviour remained unchanged. Angela did not know what else to do. She was very sceptical about contacting a behaviourist – surely she had tried everything, so what more could be done? She could no longer cope with Max's aggression but she knew she would never be able to re-home him as he would have the same problems with someone else, someone maybe less patient than Angela herself had been. Besides he had a very good home already. On her vet's advice and as the final straw, Angela telephoned an animal behaviourist.

When Erica met Max, she saw a beautiful young dog with tremendous enthusiasm, devoted to his owner but unsure of how to do the right thing. Her first task was to work on the relationship between owner and dog. Good behaviour in the house was rewarded, with no force and no threats. Max was taught to respond to Angela because he wanted to, rather than because he HAD to. Being very responsive, Max was keen to learn and loved getting titbits for doing the right thing, rather than simply being told when he did wrong things.

Then the relationship between Max and Tess (Angela's other dog) was worked on. Max was very rough in his play with Tess and although not hurting her, he was regularly practising his bullying techniques that he wanted to use on other dogs. So the solution here was to interrupt games played between the two dogs and for Angela to play with them separately. Max was to learn fun and games involved people and toys, not other dogs.

Next, outside work began. Max loved chasing after toys but no-one had ever taught him the rules of the game. He was now taught that even if he was chasing after his toy, if his owner called, then he must leave that toy and return to her. He could be confident in the knowledge that Angela would then produce an even better toy for them to play with.

Max always loved his toys but the aim was to get him even more keen on one toy. This "special" toy was kept out of his way for most of the time and only became available for special play times. As dogs usually want what they cannot have, this worked well.

Everything was going well but Erica felt they needed a little extra help. Toys were fine, Max said, when there was nothing else, but if other dogs were near, he still became a little distracted. So food was added as an extra reward. Max decided someone who had food AND a special toy, had to be more interesting than any other dog!

Gradually all the hard work paid off. Max learnt that the presence of other dogs meant that his mistress had something really special for him and therefore it was in his own interests to keep his eyes on her!

No force or unpleasantness had been used - that would have made the problem worse. Max had simply learnt an alternative behaviour.

Each month Erica has a dog walk for all the owners and their dogs who attend her classes. After a short while she invited Angela and Max to join her. For the first walk, Max stayed on the lead. He behaved perfectly, even when other dogs tried to push him out of the way to investigate the liver Angela had in her hand. A month later, Max and Angela joined the walk again. This time Max was off his lead, running around with a large group of dogs unknown to him.

Max now competes regularly with his mistress in obedience and agility shows. He loves to work, is happy and relaxed, loves attending dog clubs and now has his own 'dog' friends. He still needs to be controlled – Angela could not just let him off the lead in a park full of strange dogs and forget about him; he might be fine or he might not – she does not want to find out. But as long as she has his toy, Max keeps his attention on his mistress.

Angela has been 'absolutely thrilled' with her dog's progress. The change was 'wonderful'. He is now a completely different dog and lovely to own. How thankful she is that he was given a final chance.

Erica says: 'I recently saw Max working. He was running full blast across the ring with tremendous enthusiasm. He picked up his dumbbell and ran back to Angela to sit happily in front of her. I don't know about the accuracy of the exercise. I didn't notice. All I saw was Max being happy and full of enthusiasm and fun, running off his lead in a field full of other dogs. The other dogs might as well not have been there – Max only noticed his mistress and his toy!'

SADIE

Roamed the streets alone for three long years.
She gradually learnt to give her trust to Erica Peachey
and as a result found a whole new life.

In the world of animal abuse and neglect there are dogs who are picked up by the Police and Dog Wardens, dogs who spend their days in animal shelters and dogs rescued by the public, to be given a new loving home.

Then there are those left for years to live wild, roaming the streets – dogs like Sadie.

Ten years ago Sadie was a feral dog. She roamed the streets and the avenues, the lanes and the commons of Sheffield, out in all weathers, often seen in the distance and always alone. She was probably not born into the wild but she lived as a wild dog for three long years. She never joined up with people; she never joined up with other dogs. She was just a solitary dog – a light tan-coloured Lurcher – alone in the world.

Anyone making an effort to talk to Sadie found it impossible. The more they tried to catch her, the more frightened she became. But over the months, perhaps her diet of rabbits needed to be supplemented and she began to make her way nearer to the houses. Sadie began to raid the dustbins.

The householders who disliked dogs objected to the sight of a stray dog running free; true animal lovers became increasingly worried about what would become of the scrawny wild dog.

A kindly couple had been putting food down for her for the last six months and on one particular day, when she came up their driveway to scavenge, they managed to trap her in a garage. They reckoned with kind words and titbits, she would soon become their friend. But they were dealing with a dog used to the harsh freedom of life in the wild.

Five long days went by and they were still unable to get near to her, let alone touch her. They had given her her name – Sadie – because she had such sad, sad eyes but they were totally stumped. What could they do next?

She was under-weight, covered in scars and bites from other dogs and riddled with sheep ticks. If they handed her over to the local kennels, she would probably be put down after seven days as no original owner would ever be found. Now she had begun to rummage around the houses, if she was set free again, an anti-dog person would be bound to find a method of getting rid of her for good.

With the luck that a dog like Sadie so desperately needed, the local Bread Man in the area just happened to mention to Erica Peachey, who was working as an Animal Behaviour Consultant at the local Dog Club, Sadie's sad predicament.

Erica recalls: 'My first thought, I'm afraid to say, on seeing Sadie was 'What an Ugly Dog!' My impression of the Lurcher was one of a dog who was totally resigned. Her eyes were dull, she was covered in scars and wounds. She had the same blank anxious expression some zoo animals have.'

When Erica tried to approach Sadie, the terrified dog ran as far away from her as she could. That was on her first visit and there was not much improvement on their second encounter. Expecting Sadie could well bite, Erica cornered the dog to put on a lead and collar. Sadie did not bite but went absolutely crazy at the sight of a lead. She bit the lead until her mouth bled.

Erica returned several times to visit but made little or no progress. Realising she was getting absolutely nowhere and knowing she had to do something – in her words – 'I was her last hope' – she put the lead on the dog and walked her back to her own home.

'The seven miles took a very, very long time,' Erica recalls. 'But we worked a few things out.' Sadie resigned herself to

SADIE : *'On our journey home, Sadie lay in the grass and refused to move.'*

wandering behind as long as Erica did not turn around and look at her. If Erica spoke, she would pull backwards. Every chance the dog had, she lay down in the long grass and refused to move. She had no interest in any titbits. The hours went by. 'She made it quite clear that this was not what she wanted,' says Erica. 'But we made it home at last.'

From then on this sad, wild dog had an awful lot to learn. House training Sadie was Erica's worst nightmare. Sadie had probably never lived in a house before and once inside, it took a very long time for her to go back outside again. Erica's two other dogs, Mindy and Ben, both welcomed the new arrival. Ben just wanted to play and Mindy was quite prepared to be 'nice'. But Sadie did not know what 'play' or 'being nice' was.

'She was extremely wary of both dogs. Yet over the weeks Mindy and Ben helped Sadie considerably,' remembers Erica. 'She became far more confident with them than with me, her new mistress.'

Sadie was so worried and scared of Erica that when she did do something right, Erica could never reward her and telling her off was totally out of the question. When she was left, she became extremely destructive of anything that her mistress had handled, ripping it wildly to shreds. It took her a full three months to gain enough confidence to follow the other dogs outside if it meant walking around a door.

Her progress in everything was very, very slow. Erica could understand all Sadie's reactions but it worried her continually that the dog was just so nervous and so desperately unhappy. She says: 'I had owned her for a full year before she ever wagged her tail at me. It was a VERY long year!'

When Erica had first brought Sadie home, her intention had been not to keep her but to re-habilitate her and then find her a caring, new home. But she says: 'I have only ever re-homed one dog and I cried solidly for three weeks afterwards! It is hardly surprising Sadie never moved on!'

Ten years on and Erica has learnt a lot about her friend. Sadie has learnt a lot too. She knows Erica will look after her and that there is no need for her to scavenge and be quite so independent. Erica states: 'She is like no other dog that I have ever met and I know not to expect her to react in the way other dogs would.'

Three years ago Sadie's story nearly ended in tragedy. Erica went abroad for a couple of days to give a seminar and Sadie and Eko (Erica's new puppy) were looked after by a friend. When the friend visited someone in the centre of Liverpool, a door was left open, Eko wandered out and Sadie followed. As the friend panicked and ran after them shouting, Eko returned but Sadie shot off in the opposite direction. Sadie disappeared.

An awful few days followed of walking the streets, asking everyone and putting up posters and adverts everywhere. Erica says: 'After a while, I honestly thought that Sadie's luck had run out. She had been in a busy area, unknown to her and had absolutely no chance of finding her way to anywhere familiar.' Bonfire night came and went and Erica, in despair, really thought that was it. 'After all we had gone through together, I

SADIE : 'I cannot look at Sadie without feeling so relieved and so proud of her'.

thought it so unfair to all end like this.'

However, in Toxteth city centre there was a block of flats with a security door which had been vandalised. A lady living there came across Sadie, trembling in a corner, blood coming from her feet. She kindly took her in, telephoned the RSPCA to enquire how to bandage a foot, cooked her some liver – which Sadie was too frightened to eat – and managed to contact Erica.

When Erica arrived, Sadie was in a terrible state. She was shaking all over, her feet were in an awful mess and she wouldn't look at her mistress or move at all.

However, with a few days rest and care, Sadie was back to normal, fully fit and along with Erica, extremely happy. 'I cannot say how pleased I was,' says Erica. 'I still cannot look at her without feeling so relieved and so proud of her.'

Sadie is still very easily worried but she has become extremely well behaved. 'I'm not saying she's perfect,' admits Erica. 'But most of the time she's fairly near!' She joins in all the activities and travels everywhere with her mistress – visiting playgroups to teach children how to approach strange dogs, to clubs for talks, visiting friends – everywhere! She has learnt to relax and still plays with the exaggerated movements of a young puppy, acting younger than she did several years ago. She still rarely wags her tail at anyone other than Erica, although she has several dog and human friends now. If she likes someone and wants attention, she will stand a few feet away from them and wait. If they do not respond to her, then she will go away again. With her mistress it is different:

'When Sadie comes and gently pushes her nose against my leg, I know we have achieved something together.'

TUFTY

*A tiny Chinese Crested dog, full of fear. Endless patience
by FRESHFIELDS ANIMAL RESCUE CENTRE
gave him his chance.*

Tufty, a tiny Chinese Crested dog, was found alone in a house
with his dead owner. He had been a stud dog in a kennel for
eight long years, then sold to an elderly lady who had died
within six months.

Tufty was terrified by the whole ordeal. In pure fear he had
bitten the man who had tried to rescue him and by a piece of
luck was brought to the Freshfields Animal Rescue Centre in
Liverpool.

Lesley Tarleton remembers: ' He was brought in to me, an
obese, terrified, little creature, looking like a cross between a
pot bellied pig and E.T.!'

Poor, ugly Tufty, quivering with fear, immediately took
refuge under Lesley's bed. But no amount of cajoling would
tempt him out and there he stayed for almost TWELVE
MONTHS!

He would venture out only to eat and do his toilet on the
newspaper. Many a time Lesley thought it would be kinder to
put him to sleep, after all it was no life for him, living like that
under the bed. Each time she made the decision, she would give
him 'just one more week to see if he would come round.'
Weeks went by – another death sentence – then 'just one more
chance; maybe just one more week.'

Then the miracle that Lesley had been so desperately waiting
for, happened. Tufty plucked up all his courage and actually
came out from under the bed whilst Lesley was still in the
room. What a wonderful day!

And very slowly, the tiny little dog gradually improved.
Once day he would let Lesley stroke him; another day he would

sit on her lap – albeit rigid with fear! But it was an improvement. Each step he made was so exciting. Lesley had waited so
long for Tufty to be her friend. She dared not remember the
number of times she had so nearly given up.

With courage, Tufty learnt to cuddle up to Lesley, wag his
tail and behave almost like a normal dog. He was still very shy
of other people but Lesley now knew she would never part with
him – he would pine for her if he were to go to a new home.
And besides, Tufty had made another new friend too – Mr.
Whippy, an eleven-year-old Greyhound who was taken to be
destroyed by his owner and managed to get a reprieve when
Lesley stepped in.

True animal lover Lesley says: 'Both will stay with me until
they die. They've both had hard lives and need stability,
patience and constant reassurance.' Lesley has more than
proved she has the patience!

TUFTY : *A tiny Chinese Crested,*
who found it hard to trust anyone.

CANDY & NIPPER

*Two special rescue dogs, given their chance
in the hands of an Animal Healer.*

One November, several years ago, a fifteen-month-old yellow Labrador/Retriever, named Candy, was rescued from the RSPCA to join up with a dog-loving couple, Freda and Tom Bowers. She was the size of a small pony, with the energy of a wild horse and throughout the winter Freda and Tom found themselves walking marathons through every field and wood! 'Don't let her off the lead until she is used to you,' said the RSPCA so Freda hung on to the end of a long length of washing line with all her might, as Candy hauled her through all the squelchy muddy puddles that she came across! But gradually, they managed to train her and she soon settled into her three walks a day.

'But the following Spring,' says Freda, 'Candy started to stand on three legs, lifting her left hind foot off the floor.' The vet's first impression was that she had twisted her knee.

The condition worsened quickly and several x-rays later, Candy was diagnosed as having acute osteo-arthritis – the youngest case the vet had ever seen. A surgeon from the Veterinary College recommended surgery – to cut the muscles and relieve the pain but this would leave her with a stiff leg.

'By this time Candy could only walk about two hundred yards before having to lie down and rest. Her hip joint was visible through her fur and all her flesh seemed to have left her hip,' says Freda. 'We were at a loss as to what to do.'

A surprising chain of events were about to follow. Freda and Tom were offered a "surprise" holiday in a Devon holiday home. Freda remembers: 'With only four days notice, we were busy getting ready. So, with no time to sit and watch television after work, it was lucky – or strange - that whilst preparing dinner in the kitchen, I heard a lady being interviewed about her Airedale, on the 'Nationwide' television programme. She claimed her dog had been made well by a healer who "specialised in healing animals". I dashed to the television to see who was speaking and just managed to catch the name of the Healer – a Marilyn Preston of Saltash in Cornwall.'

As soon as her husband emerged from the garden, Freda told him excitedly what she had heard and since Saltash was only twelve miles from their holiday home, they agreed to try to find the healer once they were down in Devon.

Freda and Tom spent the whole of a Sunday morning touring Saltash, asking everyone in the shops, in the streets, anywhere and everywhere, if they knew of an 'Animal Healer called Marilyn'. Just about to give up, they tried one last shop – 'Yes', here they knew Marilyn and 'Yes', they had an address!

Living quietly in Saltash, Marilyn Preston Evans was spending many hours helping every animal in need. She originally had a small Spiritual Healing Hospital for wild birds and animals and as word of her work spread - through relieved pet owners – she began to care more and more for the helpless creatures that found their way to her home. Providing relief through the healing power working through her, working on contact healing by the laying on of hands, or on absent healing and making full use of Bach Flowers, all over Devon and Cornwall, owners and their pets were having good reason to thank her. Within no time, she had had to place a small sign over her gate: "No more animals and birds taken in through lack of space!"

Freda and Tom poured out their story to Marilyn. 'Was there anything, at all, she could do for their Candy?'

Freda remembers: 'Candy loved people – any human being was her target for fussing, parading round and round like a circus act, but within a few minutes, Marilyn had her in a deep sleep for about twenty minutes – we had never seen her so

CANDY : *With the help of an Animal Healer, she once again enjoyed her romps in the countryside*

quiet!'

Candy visited Marilyn twice more that week before Freda and Tom had to return home to Hertfordshire.

'We noticed *some* improvement in Candy and planned to return to Saltash, later in the year – which we did – for another visit to Marilyn.'

'During the winter a *definite* improvement was obvious. She began to walk further before having to rest. Her flesh began to cover her bony hip joint and although she had "bad days", most of the time she was much better.'

'The following year we returned to Devon in the Spring, by which time Candy was capable of quite long walks and she was now looking absolutely normal around the hip. This was our last personal visit to Marilyn as we moved further north but Marilyn kept Candy in her thoughts and we kept in touch by letter.' Once settled in Derbyshire, both Freda and Tom became very involved in rescuing animals and spend much of their time helping at The High Peak Dog Rescue at Sparrowpit.

As for Candy – 'When she reached the grand age of fifteen, she could still walk further than she could before we "found" Marilyn! We will always be so grateful to her for saving Candy's life for us – she says she didn't do anything – but she is the only person we can see to thank.'

§

Like Candy, Nipper was also to find help in Marilyn's hands. Coming originally from hunting kennels, Nipper found himself rescued by animal lovers Sheila and Ron King. 'Nipper did not have the aggression needed for hunting and was about to be destroyed so we took him home as a pet when he was about eighteen-months-old.'

All was well until October '95. Whilst out for his morning walk, Nipper suddenly found himself attacked by two Boxer dogs. He lay on the ground, twitching in seizure. But he seemed to recover well.

About three weeks later however, Sheila noticed Nipper seemed to have something wrong with his eyes. 'He was squinting in the light and the whites of his eyeballs had turned red. He had difficulty climbing steps and kept bumping into obstructions. We took him straight to see the Senior Partner at the Veterinary Surgery, who thought the problem had been caused by cement dust.'

After a week of treatment with an eye ointment, Nipper became completely blind. The treatment was altered to include eye drops plus water-reducing tablets and Sheila and Ron arranged to visit an Eye Specialist at Tavistock.

'The Specialist explained that Nipper had suffered a trauma after being attacked and fluid had built up at the back of the eyes. The pressure of the fluid had detached the retinas and these were floating around loosely in the eyeballs. The Specialist gave us additional tablets to try to relieve the pressure but there was no guarantee the retinas would go back into place. We were warned we may have to take him to Newmarket, the only centre in this country for animal laser treatment and there was no certainty even this would succeed. We had to come to accept our dog may be permanently blind.'

By now, Sheila and Ron had become desperate. It was becoming increasingly difficult to exercise and feed Nipper. He was bumping into everything. He was unable to distinguish night from day and he wanted to go on walks at 3 o'clock in the morning!

'We suddenly remembered Marilyn,' says Ron. 'We gave her a cross-section drawing of the eye at the start of the session. It was a copy of the drawing done by the Specialist when he explained the problem to us. From then on it was between Marilyn and Nipper.'

'Marilyn did not have an easy task as Nipper is a very lively dog and would not settle for long. At times he would go quiet and we realised that Marilyn was getting through to him at

NIPPER : *The little dog helped by healing hands.*

these periods. We had the impression that a Healer helped a patient by triggering off some sort of self-healing facility. In this case, however, Nipper did not know what was happening to him but responded to Marilyn's healing completely.'

After two sessions with Marilyn, the vet inspected Nipper's eyes. Using his pencil light, there was no reaction at all – just total blindness.

After a third session with Marilyn, the retinas had gone back into position. Nipper could see again! 'Nipper's vet was absolutely amazed and puzzled,' says Sheila. 'The Eye Specialist was *MOST* surprised!!'

'I am not remarkable,' says Marilyn, 'Nor are the powers "mine". They can be shared by all of us. I, like many other Healers, have been greatly privileged in being instrumental in bringing about literally hundreds of what would normally be termed "miracles" – but really I feel that is what *should* happen.'

'If you ask me: "How do I do it?" – I don't!

"How does it happen then?" – I haven't the foggiest!!'

SNIPER

A German Shepherd, abused and damaged.
THE LAST CHANCE ANIMAL RESCUE
came to his aid. They offered him time, love and patience.

Usually placid and friendly, Sniper, a German Shepherd, was spotted one October night lying at the side of the road, outside his owner's home on a local housing estate in Kent. He was snarling, growling, ferocious and unapproachable. His owner's response: 'He is of no use to us anymore.'

Armed with a rope, Sylvia Wragg from The Last Chance Animal Rescue in Edenbridge, Kent, was the only person willing to approach the dog. With eyes full of mistrust and hate, seven-year-old Sniper snapped and pulled away, snarling and shrieking with fear, so used was he to previous whipping and kicking.

Sylvia could not tell whether he was in shock or pain but she knew she had to help him. So, plucking up the courage, she managed to capture the snarling animal and pulled him into her van. By the time they reached the Rescue Centre, Sylvia was under a constant attack from this large ferocious dog.

Sniper was placed in a corner kennel to calm down. Three days later he was still unsettled and only very occasionally would he pick at his food. Still no-one could approach the dog – except Sylvia. Anyone taking the slightest step towards his kennel, was given a wild snarl in warning.

But Sylvia is a true animal lover. She was prepared to give this dog, like all the rest, her time and all of her love and patience.

Ever so gradually the German Shepherd would allow her to stroke under his throat. She spent long hours quietly sitting with him and very occasionally his big old head would rest on her

41

lap. But then, for no reason at all, he would suddenly flare up, snarling and snapping. The trust would be gone.

Not the sort to be deterred, Sylvia gave Sniper all her attention. She became attached to him and treated him as her own. She allowed him to sleep on her settee in the daytime and at the foot of her bed during the night. Slowly but surely, he placed a small amount of trust in her but growled viciously at anyone or anything else that came too near. Never once was Sylvia rewarded by the sight of Sniper wagging his tail as if he was happy.

No vet could get near and advised destroying the animal because of his bad temper. But Sylvia knew otherwise. She was adamant she would never let an animal die without giving it a chance; she just had to fight for Sniper – no-one else would. Besides she could see glimpses of trust in his eyes. Neighbours on the housing estate where he had been found, had already vouched for his original placid temperament and good character. So what had gone wrong? Sylvia knew something had happened. There just had to be a reason for all that anger.

Sylvia had noticed during the week that when Sniper walked his movements had been stiff. One day as he tried to climb onto the settee, he fell back whimpering in pain. She rushed off in search of another vet. Jointly they decided to anaesthetize Sniper and check him over thoroughly. He had his hip X-rayed and nothing could be found to be wrong. His spine was then closely examined.

Three six-inch nails were found along the side of his spine. There was only one way they could be there – they must have been hammered into his body. They had narrowly missed his spinal cord. The vet reckoned that the dog would have had to have been held down while nails were specifically driven in with the force of a hammer.

The nails had rusted and caused a terrible infection contaminating his whole body. There was nothing more Sylvia could do. She had to put him out of all his misery. It was

SNIPER : *'In big, sad eyes there flamed real fright, no strength was left within to fight.*
His chance had been to find a friend, to help him reach a peaceful end.'

heartbreaking for her and her rescue team but it was the kindest choice for Sniper. He would never have to face man again – owners whom he had loved and once trusted who had so badly let him down.

At least by finding Sylvia he had found a human being who cared. He had at last been able to give his trust to her. She wished more than anything she could have given him something more in return. But she did give him all her love in the last three weeks of his life. 'Each time Sniper had growled ferociously and snapped, it was because he had been wincing in pain,' says Sylvia. 'He was so very, very brave.'

The owners never admitted to the suffering caused to their dog. They did not care; they did not want to know. Sylvia had heard that they had abused their other pets, their cats, but the RSPCA was powerless to act with just hearsay as evidence.

Sniper had been let down but he did manage to find love and trust, albeit briefly, before the end. As The Last Chance Animal Rescue Centre's motto states:

'The greatest gift we will ever learn is to love and be loved in return.'

SHEBA

The 'Bouncing Dog' who kept returning to
THE MID SUSSEX HAPPY BREED DOG RESCUE SOCIETY.
Each time, they gave her another chance.

Staff at The Happy Breed Dog Rescue Society nicknamed Sheba: "The Rubber Dog". She was a loveable hound who just kept bouncing back!

Sheba, a Beagle/Labrador cross was full of fun and mischief and by the age of four months was far too energetic for her owners, who lived in a flat with no garden. So, before long, she found herself in the hands of the staff at the rescue. They were more than happy to look after her for a couple of months. Very soon a good, new home was found for her in Worthing.

Four weeks later, who should be back at the rescue, standing on their doorstep, but Sheba. She had growled at a child who had tried to take her bone away and the owner wanted nothing further to do with her.

A fortnight later, the happy, full of life dog, went off wagging her tail to another new home, this time in Burgess Hill. She stayed there four weeks, only to be returned – not for growling this time but for her 'Houdini' antics. She had become an excellent escapist!

The staff at The Happy Breed looked after Sheba for just one day this time. Then, once more wagging her tail, off she trotted to Hassocks, to a home with six foot fences! But even these fences were not high enough to keep this dog in. Seven months later – Sheba was back!

The Happy Breed could not believe it. But never to give up, within four weeks Sheba was off to get a taste of sea air at Seaford. Surely, they thought, she would soon grow out of her puppy antics? Would they be seeing her again?

Sheba stayed at the seaside for seven days. She wasn't able to get over her new owner's fences but sure as anything, she could get UNDER them!

Four weeks later Sheba found a few years settled happiness. She was chosen by an elderly couple in Burgess Hill, who loved her dearly for all her 'faults'. But after three and a half years the gentleman died and his wife was unable to give Sheba the exercise she so needed. As Lin Thurlow of The Happy Breed says: 'Our Sheba came home.'

Two weeks later, tail still wagging, off Sheba went again to Hurstpierpoint but two months later and over £300 spent to make the fences more secure, back she came!

Fortunately Sheba 'belonged to a rescue who just would not give up on her.' So...... Four months later Sheba found herself a new home in Haywards Heath and is STILL there today!! But often when the telephone rings at The Happy Breed, they wonder..... Is it the call that is asking if Sheba can come back!

There is no limit to the time dogs can stay with this rescue. Sheba, as a result, has seen a fair bit of southern England. Lin says: 'She never got upset to be returned to us. She always looked upon The Happy Breed kennel as her second home. She had the run of the farm where the kennels are and she never once made any effort to escape when she was with us.'

The rescue volunteers certainly gave Sheba her fair share of chances but her photograph, which they treasure, seems to say it all : 'There, I told you I'd be back!!'

SHEBA : 'I'm Back! So There!'

ROSIE

Cowering in a barn, waiting to be shot by a farmer's gun.
At her bleakest moment FRIENDS OF THE ANIMALS
stepped in.

One full year after Friends of the Animals helped little Spaniel Rosie, the public were still telephoning, anxious to hear she was on the mend. One enquiry even came from Australia.

Rosie is a little pedigree Cocker Spaniel bitch who spent the first eight years of her life in a shed, giving birth to a litter of pups every six months. At that time she had no name – just a number. With her last litter there had been complications and she had had to face a Caesarean. Her owner had then not bothered to take her back to the vet to have her stitches removed and her skin had grown over them.

She no longer could be used for breeding. Her owner took her across the fields to a neighbouring farmer – to be shot. Pushed into a barn, she crouched into a corner, waiting for the farmer to finish a job, before he went off to get his gun.

Luck for the first time, shone down on Rosie that day. A volunteer from Friends Of The Animals got to the farm just in time and managed to persuade the farmer to let the Spaniel go.

They called her Rosie. It was the first time she had had a name . At the Vets she sat in her pen and looked dejectedly at the floor. So they let her out and Rosie was quite content to wander around the surgery all day. Overwhelmed by all the attention, she had more love in that week than in her previous eight years. Joan Whittle from Old Hill near Dudley who has offered her help to Friends Of The Animals for many years, became her new Foster Mom and gave her all the care and love she could ask for.

Helen Sinclair of Friends Of The Animals says: 'Rosie proved to be brilliant with children and dogs. I regret we didn't get to her years ago but we found her a wonderful new home. Her new owner recently excitedly reported: 'Rosie has been on holiday to Wales, three times!' This dog was one of our many special rescues.'

In their Bearwood office a sign reads: 'It is the greatest of all mistakes to do nothing because you can only do a little. Do what you can.'

KATIE

A little Cairn, rescued from a Puppy Farm, where, used for breeding, she spent the whole of her first four years shut in an old car. CAIRN TERRIER RELIEF FUND found Katie with a dead puppy still inside her. They secured her a loving new home where Katie Cairn couldn't be happier.

From a puppy farm in Wales I came,
I had no love, no life, no name.
My days were long, cold and sad,
my master he was very bad.
Shut in a car from morn 'til night,
afraid to bark, cry or bite.
My puppies taken all away
to add more misery to my day.
No-one will care if I live or die,
if this is life, I wonder why?

Then suddenly my rescue came,
these kind people knew I was not to blame.
I'm loved to bits in every way
and kissed and cuddled every single day.
At last, the past I can leave behind
and I love my new parents who are ever so kind.
So thank you Cairn Rescue for doing this deed
and giving me all this love that I need.
Never again will my life be in vain
and I will always be grateful that my rescue came.

Extract from: KATIE by J.K. Leese
Proud owner of Katie Cairn.

KATIE CAIRN : *In her favourite chair. Her days at the puppy farm, shut in an old car, well and truly over. She now lives with a caring family and best friend 'Benji'.*

PODGE

*The 'Lowry' Dog. His hours left to die in a black bin
bag, turn to days of fun amongst the Scottish heather.*

'They managed to persuade me, by female logic (and a little
wine!) that I would love to own another dog.' – How Michael
Barton gave a whole new meaning of life to young Podge.

Early December, several years ago, six tiny puppies were
found crouched up together in a black plastic bin liner in
Birkenhead on the Mersey Estuary, just across the water from
Liverpool. The weather that year was extremely rough with
thick fog, frosts and snow and a young girl, working in the local
Post Office, had taken one of the puppies, hoping a customer
that day might take pity on it. But she had extreme difficulty in
finding the pup a loving new home. The other pups had been
lucky and were all taken care of but no-one wanted to know
about the little one in a very poor state and in a very weak
condition.

But fortune was on the puppy's side that night. Michael
Barton, then teaching at a school on the River Dee, had a wife
and daughter whose hearts went straight out to the tiny creature.
They also could be very persuasive! So they set to work on the
man of the house. 'Really, I was just playing hard to get –
persuasion was not difficult!' laughs Michael. The tiny bundle
was given the chance to embark on a whole new beginning.

Surprises were in store. The little black bitch turned out, on
closer examination, to be a little black dog! This discovery gave
him his name – Bodach – a Gaelic name roughly pronounced
'podger' meaning 'old man', later shortened to 'Podge'.

Podge was not injured in any way but he was seriously under
nourished and very poorly. He had gone way beyond the point
of being interested in food and his life was very much 'touch

and go'. Michael remembers: 'The poor little fellow was infested with internal parasites and was no more than a small handful of bones covered with a fluff of fur. At one end was a rat-like tail and at the other end, a pair of boot-button eyes.'

The vet reckoned Podge was about six weeks old, although this was hard to believe as he appeared more like a kitten than a pup.

The day the Bartons took Podge into their car, they had to make a one hundred mile journey to collect their son from college for Christmas. Podge, lay in his master's lap, wrapped in a towel, throughout the journey, Michael was genuinely afraid the little mite would die as he had absolutely no strength. But it made the family all the more determined that they would fight for this little dog's survival.

They already owned a wonderful Springer who, to say the least, was a little 'put out' at the sudden arrival of a tiny puppy into HER home. However, this Springer soon became a more important factor in Podge's survival. Little black Podge perked up immediately he saw his new friend, watched whatever she did and made little whimpering noises, snuggling up against her, thinking he had found his mother.

Podge was force fed with milk but showed no interest in any morsels of solid food. But on the fifth day in his new home Michael gave him some liver. That was the turning point and Podge took his first bite! Within a couple of days he was steady on his feet and on Christmas Day gave his first little bark! This, he was soon to find, was an excellent way to wake up the matronly drowsing Springer as and when he wanted a game.

Michael remembers: 'As Podge grew up he began to take on the shape and form, not so much his own as something invented by a well-known painter. Oscar Wilde said that life imitates art and in the case of Podge – this was certainly true! He had walked into our lives directly from the brush of L.S. Lowry. If you examine the canvases of the Lancashire painter, you will see Podge as he was in the first few months of his life.' 'A true

PODGE : *Playful in the Scottish Heather*

Matchstick Dog!' 'If I am ever asked by a casual passer-by about his breeding, 'Oh,' I will say, 'he's a Lowry, you know!' and as they nod knowingly or scratch a puzzled head, I watch them totter off to consult their A to Z of Dogs!!'

At six months Podge's rat-like tail, ears and spidery legs began to take on a feathering. The Bartons moved home and Podge was introduced to the Highlands. Out on the Scottish hills, running to his heart's content, little Podge was in his element. 'He learnt his lessons in the lore of the hills when his sixth or seventh hare lashed out with his hind legs, leaving unfortunate Podge sitting in the heather a dazed and wiser pup!' As for his introduction to sheep – 'We sat in the hills and watched a large herd of sheep being driven through a high pass. Podge sat entranced at the shepherd's whistling, the sheep dogs' barking and the herd of woolly animals bleating. He watched and listened with more than mere curiosity – a reaction which revealed at least a portion of his tangled genes. I held his collar firm but he wanted to be off to do a job he had a calling for. He waited with intense interest until the last of the sheep had disappeared and then leapt into my arms, licking my ears as he always does in moments of confusion.'

Michael is unable to say whether anything from those first awful weeks of Podge's life has any bearing on his character. He craves affection and close contact from those he loves and gets on well with any dog prepared to join him for a frolic in the heather. As the Springer gets older, Podge keeps her on her toes by biting her stump of tail until she lollops off after him. But he is very wary of strange people and any kind of 'scolding' will turn him sullen for days.

Michael's daughter is the only one who can use stern words on the little dog without him going into a long, long sulk. She has instilled into him any discipline that he may have. Says Michael: 'She had taught him to salute for his food and the odd biscuit. The gesture is made with his right leg – a sort of oblique 'Heil Hitler!' – and is so very instilled that I am sure

Podge does it before tucking into anything he finds to eat out on the bracken hills!'

Podge had become a loveable little dog, but – 'He is by no means a paragon of canine virtue.' says Michael. 'As a pup, he twice flooded the kitchen by chewing through the washing machine pipes. Then he got interested in electrics and chewed the plug off the TV, iron and radio. Once he had become interested in food, there was no stopping him. I arrived home to find Podge had completely changed shape having opened a cupboard and eaten a pound of raisins and a bag of pasta – he was totally incapable of movement! He's a cunning little rascal, learning to open the fridge, much to the delight of the Springer, who, acting as second in command, has twice helped him in the consumption of stolen ham, honeydew melon and a selection of cheeses the procurement of which meant dismantling a closed compartment at the back of the door. This resulted in Podge 'sending himself to Coventry' for at least two hours and we now have to tape the fridge shut whenever the 'wicked pair' are left!'

But sticky tape does not always help. Podge has also managed to destroy and eat part of the car, a pair of slippers, two soft dog baskets and two scrubbing brushes. 'He even ate a large tube of my best green oil paint,' says Michael, 'which resulted in some very artistic droppings! Not to mention a £50 vet's bill!'

Michael soon realised the acts of vandalism only happened if Podge was left alone, so the little black dog now goes virtually everywhere with his master as his constant companion. Michael earns his living painting landscapes and now living permanently in the Highlands, he and Podge wander far and wide in the Cairngorms strolling under the pines and junipers of Rothiemurchus to the arctic plateau of the lofty hills.

'On Ben Macdui,' recalls Michael, 'Podge came upon a herd of reindeer. He stood aside to let them pass. Stunned at first, he sat down with a thump on one of my boots, then jumped into

56

PODGE : *and the Springer-Partners-in-Crime*

my arms to be held in safety as they meandered over a ridge and out of sight. It struck me what a sharp contrast it was between utter abandonment in a stifling bin bag and being on nodding terms with reindeer on Britain's second highest hill. You know, never a day passes when I'm out with Podge and I think with horror what might have been and look with joy at what is – from Bin Bag to Ben Macdui – what a dog's life!'

PODGE : *A life in the Highlands.*

ST. NICHOLAS

Shot twice, he fought insurmountable odds to stay alive.
He became LIVING FREE's special Christmas gift.

Emily Jo Beard believed that justice was meant not for humans alone but also for animals. She believed in freedom and reverence for all life and that mankind has an obligation to better the lives of the animals with whom we share the earth.

Although she knew there were many shelters who did their best to find homes for their stray animals, she found many dogs were doomed to suffer euthanasia after a specific holding period.

This was not satisfactory to Emily Jo. She would not accept euthanasia as a solution for homeless and abused animals and decided to create an alternative. Without any fanfare, she undertook her mission to set up the Living Free Animal Sanctuary, in a one-hundred-and-sixty acre meadow in the beautiful mountains of the San Jacintos between San Bernardino and Palm Springs, California. Every animal that arrived at her sanctuary was rescued from another shelter on the day before it was scheduled to die. With a definite no-kill policy and no caging, all the animals found ample fenced areas to run free for the rest of their days or until a new home was found.

Today, a large antique dinner bell hangs within the grounds and there is no greater sound than its clanging and clattering. The bell's message goes straight to the hearts of all the staff, for it's ringing signals yet another dog has found a loving, carefully vetted home. But just as important, the vacancy which this adoption will leave at the Sanctuary, means a member of the shelter staff can head straight off to another shelter and rescue one more dog off "death row". The turnover must be kept going

EMILY JO BEARD *with her animal friends*

THE LIVING FREE ANIMAL SANCTUARY
in the beautiful San Jacintos Mountains

to save as many animals as possible. Presently, they are able to care for an average of one-hundred dogs and one-hundred-and-fifty cats at one time.

Emily Jo had made the decision not to take in dogs or cats from the public – there were plenty of other sanctuaries to do that. Caring for strays was not normally part of the Living Free policy.

But when a dog named Nicholas appeared on the scene, every single rule was waivered! 'We see miracles every day but some stand out..... Nicholas was our Christmas gift,' says Bobbi Lazare, Living Free's Director. 'He brought the people at this sanctuary something special – courage, spirit and a lot of love.'

Nicholas came into their lives at Christmas 1991. A young Shepherd-mix dog, he was found bleeding to death in the road by Tammi Henson, a Living Free employee. He had been shot twice. The first bullet had passed through his right foreleg and on through his left leg; he had also been shot through the right eye.

Tammi quickly contacted the owner. Nicholas' owner could not care less. He had no money to take Nicholas to the vet and no money to put him to sleep. He really didn't care anyway and was quite happy to leave his pet dog on the road to die.

It was unthinkable for Tammi to stand in the road and watch this happen. She instantly called her office and made special arrangements to take the dog to an emergency treatment room and urged the sanctuary to make 'just this one' exception and take in an injured stray. He had such tremendous spirit – she had to do her best for him. He had lost a great deal of blood but was still hanging on to life despite a good twenty-four hours spent finding his way home.

The vet found Nicholas had been very fortunate. No bones were shattered nor ligaments torn by the .22 calibre bullet. But unfortunately his right eye had been lost. The prognosis was poor but no-one took into account the devotion of the Living

ST. NICHOLAS : *A bullet took his eye but nothing removed his indomitable spirit!*

Free staff and the dog's own indomitable spirit.

The Christmas arrival's initial quiet, guarded nature became friendly, outgoing and inquisitive. His tail began to wag, his one good eye lit up and he offered everyone around him an abundance of licks and kisses. He was immediately christened, 'St. Nicholas', because of his relentless, cheerful nature as he struggled to show his appreciation to all who visited him in Living Free's clinic.

As the months passed, he was showered with love and care (and the occasional forbidden tasty treat!) until he was running everywhere, excitedly greeting visitors and trying oh-so-hard to get the Administration Building cats to play with him. During his stay, he became a part of Living Free's Special Needs programme – an outreach project to the valley's elderly and handicapped residents in convalescent homes. He was an excellent example for the handicapped. 'If you don't label people and animals handicapped, then they're not,' says Bobbi. It only took St. Nicholas a couple of days to compensate for the loss of depth perception due to the loss of his eye.

To help deter similar incidents in the future, Living Free offered a $500 reward leading to the conviction of the person who shot St. Nicholas. They were also totally prepared to provide a lawyer to take that person to trial.

When fully recovered, St. Nicholas went off to live with Lonnie Thomas, Living Free's Electronic Consultant, who was able to understand all the dog had been through. St. Nicholas still visits all his friends back at the sanctuary where he was given his chance.

'No dog could have committed any crime worth the punishment he had received. It was a miracle he survived,' says Bobbi. 'There was not a single grudge in him. I don't know how to explain the gift he has given us.'

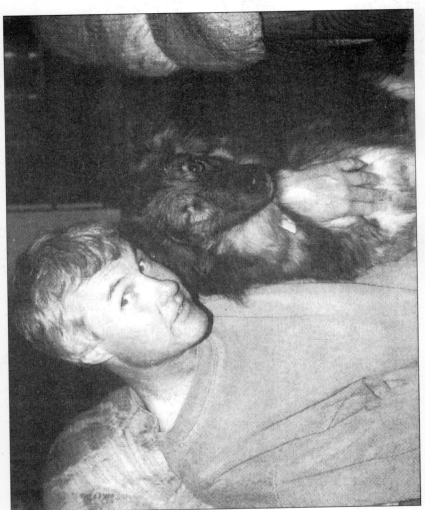

ST. NICHOLAS *finds a loving home with his new master.*

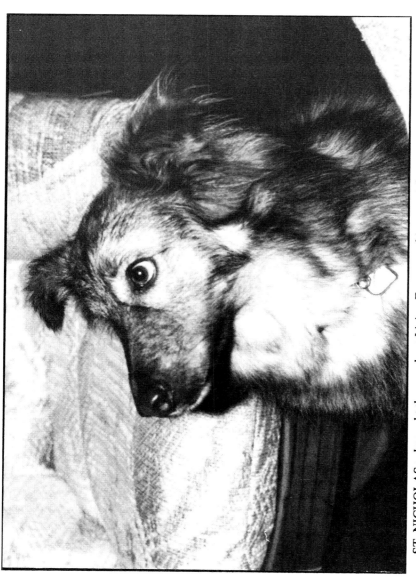

ST. NICHOLAS : *brought the people at Living Free something special – courage and a lot of love.*

©Living Free

WINNIE

Just skin and bone and dumped outside a farmhouse.
SOUTH DEVON ANIMAL SHELTER
gave her the chance she needed.

On a freezing cold November day, the local Police found Winnie. The four-year-old smooth-coated Whippet had been dumped outside a farmhouse at Rattery, Devon. She was in a very weak state, just skin and bone with her tail practically severed off and she was bleeding profusely. The gentle tempered, fragile creature came willingly to her rescuers for help.

The Police immediately made contact with the South Devon Animal Shelter at South Brent and Winnie the Whippet was rushed to the local vet's surgery.

Her tail had to be amputated without delay, although there was a considerable risk as to whether she would survive any kind of anaesthetic. For forty-eight hours this young dog's life hung in the balance – several times it was thought she would not have the strength to pull through.

For three weeks Winnie stayed in the vet's care and with an abundance of love, she gained back her confidence in mankind. She proved to be very good in the company of other dogs and despite her ordeal, had an extremely affectionate temperament. Her new chance came when she went straight from her time with the vet into a good caring new home. And there Winnie managed to reach the grand age of sixteen!

Winnie's original owner was never traced but the shelter workers did have their suspicions. A few days after she was found, a gentleman rang through to the rescue shelter wanting a Whippet. On checking his details, it was found he had given a false name and address. They believed it was Winnie's owner, who took fright when he realised the shelter would only hand

WINNIE : *Embarking on a new life*

over the dog if the home was checked. He probably realised he would have had many questions to answer from both the shelter and the Police as to how Winnie had come by her horrendous injuries.

The Chairman of South Devon Animal Shelter, Mrs. Joy Clift, says of Winnie: 'Winnie was a special dog. Despite the dreadful neglect she had received before she was rescued, her trust and determination to survive shone through the ordeal of surgery which had to be undertaken.'

ROCKY

*Confined to pace a tiny concrete pen. Subjected to immense
physical and mental suffering. His owner – fined a mere £50.
But the RSPCA gave Rocky his chance.*

The temperature had topped 80 degrees F. and the sun burnt
down, scorching the concrete base of the dog's pen. In the rear
of an Ipswich back garden, pacing back and forth inside the
wire enclosure, was Rocky. Confined for months, day in, day
out, Rocky the black German Shepherd, oblivious to life, paced
up and down.

The enclosure, 10ft.6ins. long and 5ft.10ins. wide, fenced to
a height of 4ft.6ins. had no gate. Stale excrement covered the
concrete base, the whole pen giving off a stale and pungent
aroma. Two empty bowls stood in the corner. Initially for food
and water, they had become dirty and dusty – signs that they
had not been filled for some time.

Following up a call from a member of the public, RSPCA
Inspector Ron Summers entered the back garden and
approached the enclosure. There was no reaction from Rocky;
no excited wagging tail at the sight of human company. The dog
appeared as if transfixed, almost totally devoid of spirit, contin-
uing to pace back and forth, up then down.

A dry, rough, patchy coat, with much fur missing, covered
his emaciated body. He was so underfed, his rib and pelvic
bones were all clearly prominent. As Ron Summers lifted the
animal from its enclosure, a confused and uncertain Rocky,
with all four legs splayed outwards, collapsed in a heap.

Unable to track down the owner, Ron called in Police assis-
tance. With Ron, Rocky had found a friend. He was taken to the
RSPCA Martlesham Animal Home where he ate hungrily,
drank profusely and was thoroughly examined. The vet stated

ROCKY : *Emaciated and left to pound back and forth all day in a concrete pen.*

©RSPCA

that this pathetic animal was 'in the worst mental state' he had ever seen.

Rocky had weighed 51lbs. when he was rescued but within forty days he had reached the normal weight for a large framed German Shepherd dog.

As is usual with the RSPCA, lengthy investigations took place. The owner was taken to Court but denied causing his pet any unnecessary suffering. He had told Police that it was up to his two sons aged nine and thirteen to feed Rocky, otherwise they would not get any pocket money. He reckoned his dog had been ill, probably through rat poisoning. As far as he, the owner, was concerned, his dogs WERE getting food.

The owner was fined a mere £50 by the town magistrates for neglect. An RSPCA request, to disqualify him from keeping animals, was rejected.

At the time of Rocky's rescue, Ron Summers had been an RSPCA Inspector for twenty-one years. He can say in all honesty that he has seen countless dogs in pens and enclosures. But the memory of Rocky, pacing up and down, oblivious to life, will stay with him forever. He felt Rocky had been subjected to 'the most horrendous physical and mental suffering imaginable.' These words are from an Inspector who had seen a multitude of cruelty and animal abuse.

Rocky still bears the scars. He is still nervous of strangers but he has a new life now in a loving, new, Ipswich home. His new owners think he is 'The Best Dog in The World – A Beautiful Animal.'

ROCKY : *Fully recovered in a loving home.*

LOUIS

A Special Rescue by WOOD GREEN ANIMAL SHELTERS

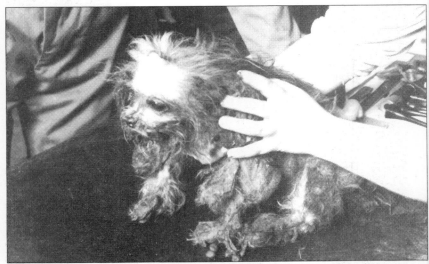

LOUIS : *Fragile and frail, his coat encrusted with excrement.*

©Wood Green Animal Shelters

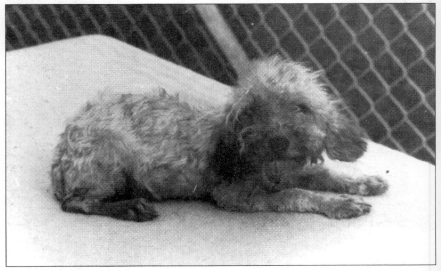

LOUIS : *A little tender care and his eyes begin to sparkle.*

©Wood Green Animal Shelters

LOUIS : *A very happy Poodle,*
so proud to have been given a chance

ABBE

*Never allowed outside; fed on a diet of nothing
but sweet biscuits for two whole years.
THE ANIMAL SAMARITANS were there to help.*

Abbe, a two-year-old fawn and brown Lurcher, was found living in filthy conditions in a flat near Catford, South-East London. She had never been outside in her life. She had never been fed on anything other than sweet biscuits.

Age Concern, who were called to the owner's home, found the owner threatening to have the dog destroyed. So, immediately they contacted the London based charity Animal Samaritans.

Having visited the house, an Animal Samaritans member commented: 'The conditions this dog were kept in were unbelievably dirty. Her owner had never cleaned up after her. We had to change our shoes when we left.'

Poor Abbe weighed half her proper weight, her skin and fur were in a very poor condition and she was immediately treated by a vet. She gradually made good progress but after her horrific two-year experience, it was considered unsuitable to re-home her in a family with children. With the help of Greyhound and Lurcher rescue, Abbe finally went off to a new, very caring home.

Receiving no grants or legacies, Animal Samaritans rely totally on fund raising and public support and every donation they receive is spent directly on animals in need. Cruelty cases can prove out of their province, as they have no jurisdiction in law to become involved. But their name says it all – "Animal Samaritans – there to help, to deal with the lost, the thrown-outs and the unwanted." Without kennels or sanctuary, all rescued animals are fostered in private homes and no animal is ever put to sleep unless it is suffering from a terminal illness.

ABBE : *The Animal Samaritans came to help.*

The volunteers spend their time vetting new homes and have now become a vast growing group of dedicated animal lovers who manage to rescue and re-home over two-hundred dogs and puppies, two-hundred cats and kittens, and a hundred rabbits within a year. They feed a numerous collection of unwanted strays and release many, many injured wild birds back into their habitat.

'Lovely to look at, delightful to hold – and a commitment for life.' 'If a lot of people thought that way,' say the Animal Samaritans, 'our work would be cut in half.'

SNOBY

A dog caught in the mess of a divorce.
St. Bernard lover Hilary Flint came to his rescue and so began
THE ST. BERNARD TRUST.

Snoby "Finetime Whatchamacallit" – a very grand name for a very special St. Bernard. His rescue was the catalyst to the formation of The St. Bernard Trust. If Hilary Flint had not become involved in helping Snoby, The Trust as a registered Charity, may never have begun.

In 1984, Hilary with her husband Phil, a Fighter Pilot in the RAF, found themselves posted to Pembrokeshire. Living temporarily in a married quarter, until they were able to sell their own Norfolk cottage, Hilary would walk her two beautiful St. Bernard bitches – Sadie and Sophie – on the nearby disused racecourse.

On one particular day, she struck up a conversation with a fellow dog walker – an American Serviceman's wife – walking her own St. Bernard 'Schnorbitz'. The dog had come from a newsagent in Llanelli, who had been too busy to take him out for walks. Hilary noticed, on that first meeting, that Schnorbitz had a nasty sore on his side. When she suggested that a visit to the vet might be a good idea, she was amazed at the response: 'Oh, I can't afford to take him to the vet,' came the Alabama drawl. This was swiftly followed up by a further comment: 'Ooh! Wouldn't it be just woooonderful if we had some puppies together..... Oooh! I want a puppy!' Needless to say the two comments did just not go together and Hilary was not impressed.

She would frequently see the American lady parading Schnorbitz up and down the racecourse and occasionally she would hear how the great dog had broken loose and charged in

76

'FINETIME WHATCHAMACALLIT' *better known as* SNOBY
the beautiful St. Bernard who helped to set The St. Bernard Trust in motion.

through someone's open front door, knocking the poor resident cats for six by the sudden appearance of a huge wolf in their home! Or how Schnorbitz had got out of his garden, entered the neighbour's property and spent the rest of the morning having a wonderful time pulling the washing off the line.

Time went by and Hilary and her husband finally moved into their new home and Hilary scarcely thought about Schnorbitz. Until one day, for some strange reason, while she was reading the paper , she found her eyes straying towards the names under the list of divorces. Quite why she did that on that day she will never know! There in front of her eyes, Schnorbitz's owner, with her address in Ohio, simply stood out amongst the list. Hilary's immediate thought, as all dog lovers will understand, was what would have happened to Schnorbitz? If his mistress had returned to the USA and he was living with his master who worked all day, who would be looking after him?

Not knowing what she was going to say but acting purely on impulse, Hilary drove up to Schnorbitz's home. She could just about see his large head peering out from a huge barricade of junk, planks and bicycles pressed up against the gate to stop his escape. As she rang the doorbell, the face of an Alsation scowled at her through the window!

The door was opened by the American Serviceman's new girlfriend. Hilary managed to explain that as she had two St. Bernards of her own, she was concerned that she had not seen Schnorbitz recently. The reason given by the girlfriend, worried her immensely. 'He doesn't come in; he slobbers all over you and mucks up your clothes. He lives in the shed now.'

The 'shed' turned out to be the small type of potting shed heaped with filthy bedding and a garbage bin. Hilary could see Schnorbitz outside the kitchen door - watching her but not moving. He knew he must *never* enter the house.

Hilary had seen enough. She gathered, on speaking to the next-door neighbour, that Schnorbitz never went for walks now and his food was passed to him over the wire fence. He was fed when someone 'remembered' and the neighbours often heard him banging the door and barking because he was so bored and hungry.

An RSPCA Inspector was unable to help Hilary since the dog had food and shelter. The only step she could think of was to offer to buy Schnorbitz. The owner was only too keen – and demanded £300! But somehow he found out that Hilary was the one responsible for contacting the RSPCA, so immediately changed his mind and decided she could not have Schnorbitz at *any* price.

Somehow Schnorbitz had to be rescued. Hilary finally persuaded a dog-loving friend to call on the owner and wave £100 cash under his nose. Out she came – accompanied by a flea-ridden Schnorbitz with his dirty feeding bowl! Schnorbitz never went anywhere near that home again.

Firstly, Schnorbitz had his name changed to 'Snoby' and he began a new life with Hilary, Phil, Sophie and Sadie. He fell instantly in love with these two bitches and would sit licking their faces and ears all over! He had great difficulty adjusting to the fact that he was allowed inside this house. He would sit slobbering at Hilary's kitchen door just looking in, not daring to put a paw over the threshold. Even if the door was left slightly ajar, he never attempted to push it open. But as the days went by, he began to realise that he was welcome inside to join Sophie and Sadie. Hilary found he had not even been house-trained, so she spent her time dashing round with buckets and carpet shampoo!

Snoby had been literally crawling with fleas but after a good session with the vet for worming and after a good bath, all his minor problems began to disappear.

He spent the rest of his days with Hilary having wonderful times on the Pembrokeshire beaches, going to St.Bernard Club Shows and spending lazy days splashing with Sophie and Sadie in the stream that ran alongside his garden.

Cardiac Myopathy set in just before his seventh birthday and sadly Snoby is no longer with Hilary. The sadness at his loss was immense but his memory will live with her forever.

At the time of Snoby's rescue, Hilary was a member of The United St. Bernard Club but after the concern she experienced over his traumas, she began to wonder just how many Saints are in that sort of predicament. Individual members of The St. Bernard Club helped in their own areas but there was no 'Rescue Officer'. So Hilary, having offered her help to any Saints in South Wales that were in need, soon found herself appointed St. Bernard Rescue Officer and very soon The St. Bernard Trust Registered Charity was formed. Hilary became the Secretary and Snoby proudly appeared on their first Christmas card and on the top of their headed notepaper.

Once the Charity was established, the rescue work just snowballed. Eight years on, they now re-home seventy to eighty St. Bernards every year, which is no easy task finding homes for the middle-aged or older adorable but very large animals. But many Saints, in years to come, can be grateful to Snoby, whose rescue will have led to their salvation.

SODA

Attacked as a three-month-old puppy by her mum;
her owners no longer wanted her.
THE NATIONAL ANIMAL WELFARE TRUST came to her aid
and have never given up on her string of illnesses.

Soda, a chocolate Doberman bitch, was barely twelve-weeks-old when she came into the hands of The National Animal Welfare Trust. She had become the last remaining puppy from a litter bred from a pet – the pup the owners had planned to keep. But disaster struck. When Soda was about three months old, she was attacked by the mother dog and the owners, instead of seeking help from a vet, simply decided they no longer wanted her.

Five days later, little Soda arrived at The Trust. She was in a great deal of discomfort, had been badly bitten around the head and there were multiple bite wounds on her ear, cheek and by the side of her eye. As she had received no veterinary treatment, the bites had become badly infected and smelt horrific. The whole of the left side of her face was badly bruised and extremely swollen. Her general condition was also very poor. She was under-sized for her age, very thin, her skin scurfy and the fur along her back was sparse. The RSPCA Inspector called out to see Soda was quite horrified by her condition.

But luckily she had found security and love in the hands of Joy Deacon, Kennel Manageress at The National Animal Welfare Trust. Immediately Soda went into their hospital unit and spent several weeks having her wounds regularly bathed and cleaned, was treated with antibiotics and fed a specially formulated diet. At first, due to the swelling and discomfort on her face, she was unable to eat solid food but with lots of treatment and loving care, she soon began to thrive. Her bite wounds

81

healed and had left her with her own special, unique, lop-sided expression!

Soon Soda was ready for a new home but within a couple of weeks Joy noticed that Soda had become uncoordinated and wobbly on her legs. The problem grew worse and after seeing a specialist, Soda was diagnosed as having Wobblers Syndrome. This is a serious condition, where pressure on the spinal cord causes imbalance. Soda's only choice was to have a major spinal operation to relieve the pressure. Without it, she would deteriorate very quickly and have to be put to sleep.

When Joy collected Soda after her operation, the young dog was a pitiful sight. She was barely able to stand and her recovery period, Joy says, 'was very hard work for both of us!' Soda had to be encouraged to walk but she was very determined. She would spend ages struggling to her feet, trying to walk a few steps to retrieve a toy or a treat. Joy says: 'She fell many, many times, was often exhausted but she refused to give in.' Every day Soda was placed in a warm bath to encourage her to move her legs, which seemed to help her. Eventually Joy was able to see day to day improvement. 'Just as well,' she says. 'Soda was growing very fast and becoming very heavy to carry!'

The chance she had been given seemed to have been worthwhile. Joy reckoned that even if her original owners had finally sought veterinary treatment for her facial injuries, it would seem unlikely they would have bothered to have her spinal problems treated and most likely Soda would have been put down. The owners were eventually prosecuted by the RSPCA and found guilty of causing unnecessary suffering to a dog and were both fined.

Unfortunately poor Soda continued to have a variety of problems. Her operation wound, which had healed perfectly, suddenly broke, not once but twice. She also had a reaction to her spay wound; she was attacked by a Staffordshire Bull Terrier which locked onto her face – she was very lucky to escape with only puncture wounds; she fractured her hip when

SODA : After a string of illnesses she still manages a lopsided grin!

she fell awkwardly and if that was not enough, she also had a blood clotting problem. She underwent a further operation around her hip and although recovery was slow, Soda was soon up charging around on her four legs again. She was not going to give up!

Then came a damaged ligament in her knee, which Joy reckons will cause arthritis in later years. But, says Joy: 'I don't look too far ahead!' She knows she has done right by giving this dog it's rightful chance.

For, once Soda began to recover from her original injuries, a very strong character began to emerge, with great determination to never give in to anything without a battle. This has obviously helped her survival.

'Soda has always been a loving dog. She loves a cuddle and now lives as normal a life as possible. She can be very naughty and is always into mischief but has a great sense of humour. She loves her vet bed and will carry it around as a form of security blanket. In the summer, she will lie out in the sunshine, spreading her bed out in a suitable spot first! In cold weather, she will demand the spot beside the office heater and make sure all the heat is directed at her!'

She lives with Joy, two other dogs and six cats, all getting on well together. Her best friend, Fly, a Lurcher at the rescue centre, went off to a new home but Soda enjoyed visiting to continue their games.

Joy has nothing but praise for her Doberman, after every illness the young dog has been through. 'Although Soda is very hard work and so demanding, she gives everything, in return for the care she has received. She is an extremely affectionate dog and it is difficult to be cross with her for long, no matter how naughty she is. Owning Soda is certainly a very different experience. She really is a special kind of dog.'

TYSON

His days were doomed when his owner believed the
tabloid reports on Rottweilers. Waiting at the vet's surgery
to be destroyed, because 'he was a Rottweiler',
TAVISTOCK ANIMAL SHELTER came to his aid.

A few years ago, the proud, majestic Rottweiler became the
tabloid journalist's best friend and the man in the street's worst
enemy.

Several front page stories of a Rottweiler attacking a child
had just recently appeared when Mary Kiser, who runs the
Tavistock Animal Shelter in Devon, was paying a visit to her
local vet. The waiting room was full but a gentleman sitting in
the far corner, with a Rottweiler laying peacefully at his feet,
was obviously being given a very wide berth by everyone.

To Mary's experienced eye, the young dog looked fit and
healthy and, genuinely interested, she struck up a conversation
whilst she was waiting and inquired what was wrong with the
dog. The reply stunned her. The gentleman explained that the
dog had done absolutely nothing wrong but he had brought it to
the vet to be destroyed. The family had read all the 'horror' stories in the newspapers and were afraid that 'since it was a
Rottweiler', it just 'might' attack them. Through no fault of its
own, the puppy had found itself to be the wrong breed with the
wrong owner and was now within minutes of death.

Mary had no second thoughts that day. She found herself
returning home to the animal shelter with an eight-month-old
Rottie named Tyson!

She kept him for several weeks to assess his temperament
and several offers of a home came in for him. Mary considered
none of these suitable. People who wished to buy a Rottweiler
as a guard dog were way out of line; an alarm would have

solved any burglar problem. She knows Rottweilers are not a breed for just anyone. Loveable Tyson would need his own family, a firm hand and a lot of love.

So an advert was duly placed in a newspaper and the replies poured in. One of these seemed ideal – a middle-aged couple with no children or other pets who had just lost their twelve-year-old Rottie. A volunteer from the local Rottweiler Rescue was sent out to check the prospective owner's home and a favourable reply was received. The couple appeared to know and understand the breed, were very responsible and would give Tyson the home he so desperately craved.

The new owner travelled to Devon from the Isle of Wight to pick up the puppy and a better match could not have been made.

Later the shelter received the wonderful news that Tyson had grown into a wonderful, mature, adult dog and had become an ideal and much loved pet.

The Tavistock Animal Shelter homes dogs and cats, rabbits and sheep. Mary has found herself rescuing dogs from Dartmoor, where people think it is easier to get away with dumping their pets. Many puppies are still farmed in the South West region and she has seen dogs crated up at Plymouth railway station to be shipped abroad.

But throughout all the sad cases, she remembers Tyson's story with affection. 'Happy rescues, like Tyson's, make rescuing all the more worthwhile.'

TYSON : *Proud to be a Rottweiler*

MOUSE

A tiny, petrified, hairless little dog, discovered in the
squalor of a closed-off room. She found a friend at
THE DOGS' HOME BATTERSEA.

The Dogs' Home Battersea, in London, often takes in dogs belonging to elderly hospital patients, at their discretion. Back in December '95, they agreed to accept a dog from the South London area, but little did they know of the sad background behind the pathetic little dog called Mouse.

Mouse's owner was hit by a car and admitted to hospital. His neighbours, hearing continuous whimpering from his flat, soon realised that he must have owned a dog. A Social Worker, accompanied by the local Dog Warden, were absolutely horrified to discover, on searching the flat, a tiny emaciated hairless little creature, terrified and quivering, amongst the squalor of a closed-off room. The dog had obviously never been out in her life. She was completely petrified.

After much coaxing, little Mouse was rescued from her deplorable situation and found a clean, comfortable kennel waiting for her at The Dogs' Home. She created much discussion amongst the staff: 'She was a kind of variety of Chihuahua (we think!).'

But poor little Mouse found she wasn't exactly the kind of dog the public were willing to adopt. She deserved her own home so much but, afraid of people, tiny and with not a hair on her body, finding a new, loving family was going to be an extremely slow and impossible process.

However, it did not take long before Mouse had won the heart of one of the staff at Battersea. Jacky Donaghy would not give up on her. She felt the little dog deserved her chance and so Mouse moved into Jacky's home.

'Mouse was by no means an easy project. It took two months to house-train her, a very long three months to get her used to walking on a lead and much, much longer to get her used to other dogs and people.'

Jacky *never* gave up and her efforts were not in vain. Today, Mouse is much podgier and after being spayed, has even sprouted a few hairs!! She lives happily now with Jacky and two other Battersea dogs, enjoying her life to the full, trotting off to work at Battersea with Jacky, each and every day!

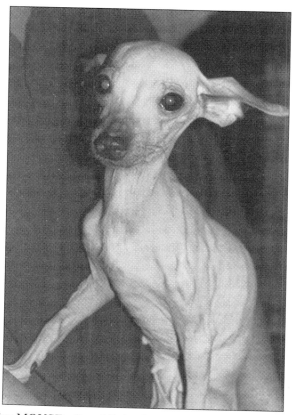

Tiny MOUSE : *Stood little chance of finding a new home until she found Jacky*

BLACKY

Her home was a squalid outhouse stinking of ammonia.
The Lancashire branch of the RSPCA came to her aid.

A call was made to the Preston branch of the RSPCA from a nearby resident, informing the Inspector that a dog had not been seen for some time and, when last seen, was very thin.

RSPCA Inspector Brian Jeffries, from the North Lancashire and Borders branch, called at the address in Wennington. There he found Blacky – a six-year-old, black/white crossbreed Labrador, emaciated, lethargic, depressed and desperate to escape her prison.

Blacky's home was a squalid, brick-built outhouse, measuring six foot by seven foot, in the rear of a garden of a semi-detached house. Brian Jeffries found that the door of the outhouse would not even open due to the clutter of household waste. He saw the dog crouched in the corner, surrounded by plastic bags, pottery, empty dog tins, bottles, disposable razor blades, an old car battery and a mass of sodden rags. There was nowhere clean or dry for Blacky to lie down. The whole outhouse stunk of ammonia fumes. Amongst the rubbish there was no sign of food nor water and it was estimated that the dog had been living in these conditions for several months.

Shaking and weak, Blacky was removed from her prison and taken straight to a vet. The majority of her skeletal structure was clearly visible and she was a staggering twenty pounds underweight. Both her eyes were very sore with severe conjunctivitis and compacted with puss, probably caused by the ammonia fumes. Her nails were overgrown, her coat dirty and she was totally de-hydrated.

At the vet's surgery, Blacky instantly drank two pints of water in three minutes flat and ate ravenously. She had suffered

BLACKY : *lethargic and gaunt*

The Door of BLACKY's *Outhouse could not open due to the clutter*

BLACKY's Home – *a deplorable, filthy shed, full of plastic bags, old furniture and stinking of ammonia*

long and unnecessarily, both by virtue of her being starved and being deprived of water and as a result of the atrocious conditions in which she had been kept.

For the next few weeks, she was given overwhelming tender love and care and a good diet to build her up. She had appeared very friendly and sociable from the outset and her faith in humanity was soon fully recovered.

In Inspector Jeffries opinion, if she had not been rescued, she would have quite simply starved to death in her deplorable home.

But, thanks to the RSPCA, Blacky – renamed Annie – found a loving new home. With her friendly nature and appealing face, re-homing was easy and she could not have been happier than with her new owners.

Her previous owner was taken to court and fined £33 plus costs and banned from keeping an animal for ten years. He admitted the outhouse 'wanted a clean out' but said: 'I was too tired after work to do it.'

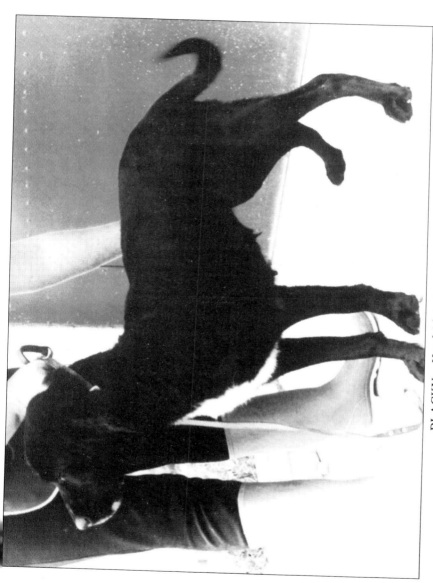

BLACKY: *Her faith in humanity, now restored*

SMOKEY

A crumpled heap with twisted paws, body and spine.
His big, brown eyes pleading. Given his chance, he became
the mascot for British based GREEK ANIMAL RESCUE.

On 26 August 1990, a car drove through the gates of an animal
shelter just outside Athens and the twisted body of what resem-
bled an Irish Setter was hauled out of the boot. The car driver
had found the dog on the side of the road and, as rarely happens
in Greece, was kind enough to transport it to the shelter.

The puppy was skin and bone. He had suffered substantial
injuries; his spine totally twisted. It looked as if he had been
struck by a car, possibly the previous week. His pitiful frame
huddled in a heap on the floor. He was pathetically thin, all ribs
and very weak and incontinent. His whole body was riddled
with ticks, tapeworm and thorns.

Vesna Jones from London, founder of Greek Animal Rescue,
looked into his big brown eyes. All she could see was the pain
and the pleading. She watched him helplessly in his efforts to
walk – one, two steps and then down he would fall, each fall re-
opening the large sores on his skin. Tears filled her own eyes
for she realised she was witnessing a typical occurrence in
Greece – yet one more animal tragedy, the kind one can witness
so often throughout Greece and it's islands.

After visiting various vets, each advising the dog should be
put to sleep, Vesna, knowing she would soon be returning to
England and that the dog would need so much care, never being
able to adapt to the hard life at the shelter, just clung on and
prayed for a miracle.

By day three, Smokey, as Vesna had named him, had had a
good bath, thorns, and grass seeds were removed from his ears
and a physiotherapist set to work stretching his muscles. He still

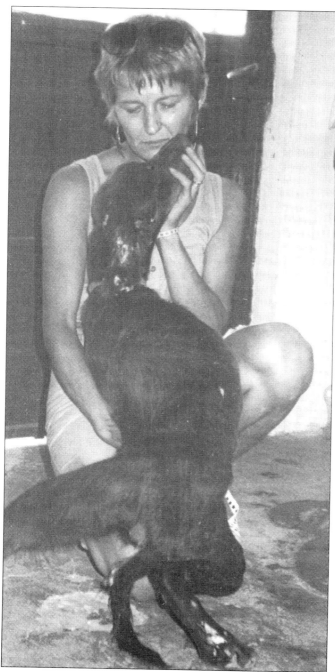

SMOKEY : *A Crumpled heap, with twisted paws begs Vesna for a chance*

could not sit down. By day six, Smokey had met Pamino, a feline playmate, and his mischievous puppy character was beginning to shine through. He had many injections to face, he was still toppling over, was 'all legs' when trying to right himself but his coat began to shine and he was beginning to show 'tremendous improvement'.

After a fun day on the beach, paddling haphazardly in the rippling water, chasing butterflies on the breeze along the sand, the time had arrived for Vesna to return to her home in London. Thirteen days of her loving care had transformed Smokey beyond recognition and now at seven-months-old he was full of zest for life. There would be simply no chance of finding 'a loving master of his own' in Greece.

Vesna knew he deserved his chance and she was not the sort to give up without a fight. At the Greek shelter she said a tearful farewell to Smokey and in the sunset that night she promised him she would see him again and would not abandon him forever.

Back in London, Vesna did not stop until she had reached her goal. She appealed in local newspapers; she organised sales and sponsored walks and with the public's amazing generosity, the large sum of money was found to bring Smokey back to England.

He completed his months in quarantine and on 'an emotional and happy day' Vesna's wishes came true and Smokey moved in with her husband, her three other dogs and her two cats. Still toppling over, Smokey would join in the games – he would just pick himself up and off he would go on yet another mad dash, only to fall flat on his face in yet another British rain puddle!

Besides the original injuries sustained in the accident – no English vet could give him any treatment as surgery on his spine and pelvis which was broken in four places would prove too risky – Smokey had another disability. His front paws are still twisted outwards due to malnutrition at birth. But each step in his immense haul back to good health, is an achievement. To sit, leaning against a wall for at least thirty seconds, was a great accomplishment. Now, seven years on: 'Smokey runs amazingly well and rarely falls over.'

Smokey's recovery has been due not only to love and care but to his great courage and determination. He now has fame in his own right and Vesna was proud to announce he was to become Greek Animal Rescue's mascot. On behalf of his four-legged friends left back in Greece, he bumbles along with several other rescued Greek dogs, taking part in dog walks and raising money in any way he can.

Vesna runs Greek Animal Rescue from her home in London. As her struggle to raise funds continues, so the work of the charity expands, helping many more needy animals. In Greece, the animal cruelty goes on – cruelty of the kind seldom witnessed here in England.

A Greek newspaper recently reported *more* complaints were received by the Greek Tourist Office from holiday makers about abuse and neglect of animals, than about the state of the hotels and the food. True animal lovers are finding they return from their holidays in Greece, not with memories of blue skies and sparkling seas but with vivid images of animals in distress. Painfully thin dogs riddled with ticks and diseases, limping from injured limbs, donkeys laden with baggage trekking up and down huge flights of stone steps from dawn to dusk with no food and no water; mules pushed over hill tops when their working life is over – the 'lucky' ones will get a shot in the head; stray cats living on tourist scraps in the summer, find no food in winter and perish; puppies sold in glass boxes on the streets sweltering in 100 degrees F. temperatures; carcasses littering deserted roads, dogs with no coats, skin raw and bleeding trying helplessly to lick themselves clean. Few Greeks believe in neutering animals. The problem will increase. Only the lucky ones find their way to the Greek Animal Rescue Shelter.

It is not easy each time Vesna returns to Britain, having spent a few days searching out the neglected, unloved creatures,

SMOKEY : *'Nothing wrong with me!'*

knowing that for every animal she has helped and brought to the safety of the sanctuary, thousands of others will die in agony. But 'It is not a matter of how many lives we have lost – It is a matter of how many lives we can save,' she says as she types charity letters and sorts out the next raffle, Smokey happily at her side.

It seems so very appropriate that Smokey should repay her kindness to him and help her to raise the funds for other less fortunate animals in the land of his birth.

CLAIRE McCLENNAN lives in Devon and works as a free-lance writer on various animal and children's magazines. She loves all animals and owns two cats – Moppet and Spangles and two Golden Retrievers – Holly and Bracken.

Another Chance is her second published book on animals.

LINDA THURLOW works as a self-taught Artist specialising in Animal Portraits. Currently she is learning silversmithing and is enjoying combining animal art with silver. She spends much time helping stray and unwanted dogs at her local Rescue Centre.

ACKNOWLEDGEMENTS

The Author would like to thank the following individuals and Animal Sanctuaries, for their help in the compilation of this book. Thousands of innocent dogs each year become victims of an uncaring world and without the never-ending, tireless efforts of true animal lovers, many dogs would not be given that vital second chance.

SSPCA – Chief Inspector Iain Keir. Edinburgh EH3 7PL
RSPCA – Inspector Ron Summers, Inspector Martin Marsh,
      Brian Jeffries. Horsham West Sussex RH12 1HG
      Publications Officer, Pippa Bush.
IFAW – David Dawson. Crowborough E.Sussex TN6 2QH
PINE RIDGE DOG SANCTUARY – Connie Cuff.
      Ascot, Berks SL5 8HJ
ANIMAL SAMARITANS – Harry Moore.
      Sydenham, London SE26 5RX
THE NATIONAL ANIMAL WELFARE TRUST – Joy Deacon.
      Watford, Herts WD2 8QH
LIVING FREE ANIMAL SANCTUARY - Bobbi and Erin Lazare.
      California 92361 USA
CAIRN TERRIER RELIEF FUND Chris Roberts.
      Barton Under Needwood, Burton on Trent DE13 8E
ST. BERNARD TRUST – Hilary Flint.
      Holyhead, Gwynedd
FRIENDS OF THE ANIMALS Helen Sinclair
      Bearwood, Warley, W. Midlands B66 4EX
FRESHFIELDS ANIMAL RESCUE – Lesley Tarleton.
      Ince Blundell, Liverpool L29 3EA
THE DOGS HOME BATTERSEA – Shirley Piotrowski.
      London SW8 4AA
THE MID-SUSSEX HAPPY BREED – Linda Thurlow.
      Haywards Heath W. Sussex RH16 1NP

GREEK ANIMAL RESCUE – Vesna Jones.
Hendon, London NW4 1PT
SOUTH DEVON ANIMAL SHELTER – Joy Clift.
Avonwick, South Brent.
WOOD GREEN ANIMAL SHELTERS.
Godmanchester, Cambs. PE18 8LJ
TAVISTOCK ANIMAL SHELTER – Mary Kiser.
Kestrel Kennels, Tavistock
LAST CHANCE ANIMAL RESCUE – Sylvia Wragg.
Edenbridge, Kent TN8 5NH
SYLPHLYKE ANIMAL SANCTUARY – Maria Goodman
Hanworth, Middlesex TW13 6QD
APBC – Erica Peachey.
Michael Barton.
Marilyn Preston Evans.
Freda and Tom Bowers.
Sheila and Ron King.
Edward Gaskell of The Lazarus Press

Front Cover photo : Jarrold Publishing

CLAIRE McCLENNAN

CELEBRITY PETS

The Dogs and Cats who brighten the lives of some of
Britain's most popular personalities — Ernie Wise,
June Whitfield, Ken Dodd, Jenny Seagrove,
Terry Waite, Anthea Turner, Kriss Akabusi, Lorraine Kelly
and many more

'A nice gentle read
about famous personalities and their pets.'
Editor, Pet Dogs.

'The book is lovely.'
Eastenders Actress, Wendy Richard

'Tis a great wee gift for animal loving pals.'
Actress, Pat Coombs.

'Absolutely delightful.
It will give us an enormous amount of pleasure
and remind us of Muffin, a perfectly lovely dog.'
World Wildlife Artist, David Shepherd.

'A lovely book.'
Radio/TV presenter, Valerie Singleton.

£6.99 RRP
Available (UK post free) from :
HolRocks Books (B), PO Box 107
Paignton Devon TQ4 7YR